Synonyms
at School

By Kathleen Connors

Gareth Stevens
Publishing

Please visit our website, www.garethstevens.com. For a free color catalog of all our high-quality books, call toll free 1-800-542-2595 or fax 1-877-542-2596.

Library of Congress Cataloging-in-Publication Data

Connors, Kathleen.
Synonyms at school / Kathleen Connors.
    p. cm. — (Word play)
Includes index.
ISBN 978-1-4339-7204-1 (pbk.)
ISBN 978-1-4339-7205-8 (6-pack)
ISBN 978-1-4339-7203-4 (library binding)
1. English language—Synonyms and antonyms—Juvenile literature. I. Title.
PE1591.C6695 2012
428.1—dc23

                                            2011052731

First Edition

Published in 2013 by
Gareth Stevens Publishing
111 East 14th Street, Suite 349
New York, NY 10003

Copyright © 2013 Gareth Stevens Publishing

Designer: Benjamin Gardner
Editor: Kristen Rajczak

Photo credits: Cover, p. 1 Szasz-Fabian Ilka Erika/Shutterstock.com; p. 5 shock/Shutterstock.com; p. 7 Morgan Lane Photography/Shutterstock.com; p. 9 © iStockphoto.com/Neustockimages; p. 11 © iStockphoto.com/bonnie jacobs; p. 13 © iStockphoto.com/Michael DeLeon; p. 15 Africa Studio/ Shutterstock.com; p. 17 © iStockphoto.com/Claude Dagenais; p. 19 SergiyN/Shutterstock.com.

Printed in the United States of America

CPSIA compliance information: Batch #CS12GS: For further information contact Gareth Stevens, New York, New York at 1-800-542-2595.

Contents

Boldface words appear in the glossary.

Just the Same

It's time to **start** the day at school! Let's **begin** by learning about synonyms.

Synonyms are words that have the same or almost the same **meaning**.

Start and **begin** are synonyms!

Hands Up

Most teachers want you to raise your hand to **talk** in class. It helps everyone pay attention if you don't **speak** out of turn.

Talk and **speak** have the same meaning. They're synonyms!

Listen and Learn

The teacher asked a question. She wants to make sure you **understand** what she's saying. Do you **know** the answer?

Know and **understand** are synonyms. They have almost the same meaning.

Working Together

When working in groups, it's important to be **kind** to others. Be **nice** to your classmates by listening to their ideas.

Are **kind** and **nice** synonyms? They are! They have the same meaning.

11

Lunchtime

There are many things to **choose** from for lunch. You can **pick** apple **slices**, carrot sticks, or even green beans to go with your sandwich! **Choose** and **pick** are synonyms!

13

Study Up

Math tests can be **hard**! However, if you listen in class and practice at home, they will be less **difficult**.

Hard and **difficult** have the same meaning. They must be synonyms!

15 + 20 = 35

18 - 5 = 13

14 + 9 =

12 - 10 =

17 + 4 =

Making Art

Learning to paint **pretty** pictures in art class is fun. You can make a **beautiful** flower or a picture of your family!

Are **pretty** and **beautiful** synonyms? They have almost the same meaning!

Shh!

The classroom is very **quiet**. It must be **silent** reading time.

Quiet and **silent** have almost the same meaning. Are they synonyms?

19

The End of the Day

Smile! Even though school is out, you get to come back tomorrow. That's a good reason to grin.

Smile and grin have the same meaning. They're synonyms!

Common Synonyms

big   ⟷   large

loud   ⟷   noisy

afraid   ⟷   scared

messy   ⟷   dirty

rock   ⟷   stone

honest   ⟷   truthful

happy   ⟷   glad

Glossary

meaning: the message behind a word or words

slice: a thin, flat piece of something cut with a knife

For More Information

Books

Cleary, Brian P. *Stroll and Walk, Babble and Talk: More About Synonyms.* Minneapolis, MN: Millbrook Press, 2008.

Fribley, Kara. *Find the Right Words with Thesauruses.* Ann Arbor, MI: Cherry Lake Publishing, 2012.

Heinrichs, Ann. *Synonyms and Antonyms.* Mankato, MN: Child's World, 2011.

Websites

Find the Synonym
www.learninggamesforkids.com/vocabulary-games/synonyms/find-the-synonym.html
Play a game to practice finding synonyms.

Index